Just for Laughs

ZOOMING, ZIPPY JOKES ABOUT VEHICLES

Julia Garstecki

ACHOO!

BLACK RABBIT BOOKS

Hi Jinx is published by Black Rabbit Books
P.O. Box 227, Mankato, Minnesota, 56002.
www.blackrabbitbooks.com
Copyright © 2022 Black Rabbit Books

Marysa Storm, editor; Michael Sellner, designer
and photo researcher

Library of Congress Cataloging-in-Publication Data
Names: Garstecki, Julia, author.
Title: Zooming, zippy jokes about vehicles / by Julia Garstecki.
Description: Mankato, Minnesota : Black Rabbit Books, [2022] |
Series: Hi jinx. Just for laughs | Includes bibliographical references
and index. | Audience: Ages: 8-12 | Audience: Grades: 4-6 |
Summary: "Through an engaging design that brings the jokes to life
with fun facts and critical thinking questions, Zooming, Zippy Jokes about
Vehicles will have readers laughing and learning"– Provided by publisher.
Identifiers: LCCN 2020016593 (print) | LCCN 2020016594 (ebook) |
ISBN 9781623107093 (hardcover) | ISBN 9781644665640 (paperback) |
ISBN 9781623107154 (ebook)
Subjects: LCSH: Vehicles–Juvenile humor. | Transportation–
Juvenile humor. | Wit and humor, Juvenile.
Classification: LCC PN6231.V36 G37 2022 (print) |
LCC PN6231.V36 (ebook) | DDC 818/.602-dc23
LC record available at https://lccn.loc.gov/2020016593
LC ebook record available at https://lccn.loc.gov/2020016594

Image Credits

123RF: Aridha Prassetya, 6; Alamy: Ivan Ryabokon, 16; iStock:
sara_winter, Cover, 11; Shutterstock: Aleksei Martynov, 4; Alex
Gontar, 17; Aluna1, 14; anfisa focusova, 4; Arcady, 7; ArtMari,
16; benchart, 6; blambca, 4; Big Boy, 7, 13, 23; BlueRingMedia,
17; Bobb Klissourski, 12–13; chompoo, 4; Christos Georghiou,
12; Danilo Sanino, 7; Danomyte, Cover, 11; dedMazay, 17; Denis
Cristo, 7, 14; elembie, 1, 11; GraphicsRF.com,
4, 20; hermandesign2015, 7; HitToon, 18–19,
19; Irina Levitskaya, 1, 18; Jon Larter, 3,
15; klyaksun, 14; Kong Vector, 16, 21;
lady-luck, Cover, 11; Linda Bucklin, 14;
Lorelyn Medina, 6; Mechanik, 1, 18;
Memo Angeles, 1, 3, 8, 9, 10, 12, 13, 16,
18, 19; Miceking, 6; newelle, Cover, 11;
Nicoleta Ionescu, 10; Pasko Maksim, 9, 13,
23, 24; Patrimonio designs ltd, 17; picoStudio,
17; Pitju, 10, 21; Pushkin, 4, 12; ridjam, Cover, 11,
14; Ron Dale, 5, 6, 10, 14, 20; Rvector, 18–19;
Sararoom Design, 12; Stockway, 16; Sujono sujono,
10; Teguh Mujiono, 1, 11, 13, 15, 23; VectorShots, 12;
Vector Tradition, Cover, 6, 16; Verzzh, 1, 3, 8, 18;
Vladislav Kudoyarov, 6, 9; Volodimir Zozulinskyi, 19;
Wimpos, 1, 15; your, 15

CONTENTS

Chapter 1
VEHICLES ON THE GO!

Traveling by plane, train, or other vehicle can be exciting. Unless your flight is delayed, of course. Or if your trip is a 14-hour car ride with your gassy brother. Yuck! If that's the case, it's a good thing you found this book! Here are some jokes about vehicles to help time zip by.

Chapter 2
BOATS, SHIPS, AND SUBS

Where do ghosts sail?

*Lake **Eerie***

Knock, knock.

Who's there?

Canoe.

Canoe who?

Canoe open the door please?

What do you call
a group of people
standing on a dock?
pier *pressure*

Fun Fact

There might really be ghosts on ships. Some people say certain boats, such as the RMS Queen Mary, are haunted!

Why do oars fall in love?

Because they're row-mantic.

What do cats use to see
out of submarines?

purr-i-scopes

What do you call a dog in a submarine?

a sub-woofer

What do you give a sick submarine?

vitamin sea

Fun Fact

Tools called periscopes let people see out of submarines. People use them to see out of tanks too.

Chapter 3

SPEEDING BY IN TRUCKS and CARS

What snakes are found on cars?

windshield **vipers**

Fun Fact
There are more than 200 kinds of vipers.

What has six
wheels and flies?
a garbage truck

Where do Volkswagens
go when they get old?
the old Volks' home

Why can't motorcycles
hold themselves up?

*Because they
are two tired.*

What kind of car do pets hate?

Cor-vets

What has 10 letters
and starts with G-A-S?

automobile

When is a car like a frog?

When it's being toad!

Chapter 4
PLANES, TRACTORS, and TRAINS

Why did the plane get
sent to its room?

*It had a bad **altitude**.*

What did the football player
say to the flight attendant?

*Put me in **coach**!*

How do rabbits
travel long distances?
by hare-o-plane

I wrote a book about planes.
It really took off.

Where does a
mountain climber
keep his plane?
*a **cliff-hanger***

How did the farmer find her sheep?

She tractor down.

Why did the farmer get his tractor stuck?

*He was plowing a **magnetic field**.*

Fun Fact

Some people think
aliens make crop circles.
Others aren't so sure.
What do you think?

What kind of robot
turns into a tractor?

a transfarmer

How do farmers
make crop circles?

with a pro-tractor

What do you call a train
that won't stop sneezing?

an achoo achoo train

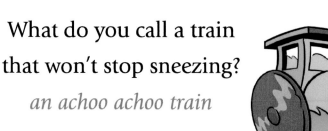

Why are railroad tracks so angry?

*Because people are always **crossing** them.*

Why was the train late?
It kept getting sidetracked.

How many jokes can
you write about trains?
*I'm not sure. It's hard for
me to keep track.*

Chapter 5
Get in on the Hi Jinx

Let's get serious for a minute. Vehicles need people to drive and pilot them. But it's **engineers** that make them! Engineers design planes, ships, and cars. They study different materials to find out which is best. Engineers make sure vehicles can stop and start. They help keep vehicles safe too. Without these workers, getting around would be pretty hard. And we wouldn't have these jokes!

Take It One Step More

1. What sounds do different vehicles make? Can you create jokes using the noises?

2. Pick your favorite joke from the book. What makes it so funny? Write a similar joke.

3. Pick a joke from this book that didn't make you laugh. How can you improve it?

GLOSSARY

altitude (Al-ti-tood)—how high a place or thing is above sea level or Earth's surface

cliff-hanger (KLIF-hang-er)—a suspenseful situation

coach (KOHCH)—the least expensive seats on an airplane or a train

cross (KROSS)—to go from one side of something to the other; it also means to turn against or betray.

eerie (EER-ee)—strange and mysterious

engineer (en-juh-NEER)—a designer or builder

magnetic field (mag-NE-tik FEELD)—an area where an object's magnetic properties affect neighboring objects

pier (PEER)—a structure that goes out from a shore into the water

viper (VAHY-per)—a type of poisonous snake

BOOKS

Seed, Andy. *The Anti-Boredom Book of Brilliant Things to Do: Games, Crafts, Puzzles, Jokes, Riddles, and Trivia for Hours of Fun.* Anti-Boredom Books. New York: Skyhorse Publishing, 2020.

Whiting, Vicki, and Jeff Schinkel. *Super Silly Jokes for Kids.* Mount Joy, PA: Happy Fox Books, 2020.

Winn, Whee. *Lots of Animal Jokes for Kids.* Grand Rapids, MI: Zonderkidz, 2020.

WEBSITES

Airplane
kids.britannica.com/kids/article/airplane/352719

Fun Train Facts for Kids
www.sciencekids.co.nz/sciencefacts/vehicles/trains.html

History of Cars for Kids
www.dkfindout.com/us/transportation/history-cars/